Contents

Small Soldiers ™

Adapted from the novelization by
GAVIN SCOTT
Based on the screenplay written by
GAVIN SCOTT and **ADAM RIFKIN**
and **TED ELLIOT**
& TERRY ROSSIO

Level 2

Retold by Geraldine Kershaw
Series Editors: Andy Hopkins and Jocelyn Potter

Pearson Education Limited
Edinburgh Gate, Harlow,
Essex CM20 2JE, England
and Associated Companies throughout the world.

ISBN 0 582 38099 5

First published in the USA by Grosset & Dunlap, Inc., a member of
Penguin Putnam Books for Young Readers, New York 1998
First published in Great Britain by Puffin Books 1998
This edition first published 1999
Second impression 1999

TM & © Universal City Studios, Inc., DreamWorks
and Amblin Entertainment, 1998, 1999
All rights reserved

Typeset by Digital Type, London
Set in 11/14pt Bembo
Printed in Spain by Mateu Cromo, S.A. Pinto (Madrid)

Published by Pearson Education Limited in association with
Penguin Books Ltd, both companies being subsidiaries of Pearson Plc

For a complete list of the titles available in the Penguin Readers series please write to your local
Pearson Education office or to: Marketing Department, Penguin Longman Publishing,
5 Bentinck Street, London W1M 5RN.

Introduction

A minute later Archer was in the kitchen. His feet were above his head, and his head was over a dangerous machine. "This is the end for you, Gorgonite!" said Chip Hazard. "Now talk! Where are the other Gorgonites?" Archer suddenly felt happy inside – the other Gorgonites weren't dead! But he said nothing.

When Globotech buys Heartland Toys, the new boss wants more exciting toys – intelligent fighting toys for children. The problems begin when his two best workers put computer chips for weapons inside the toys. The Commandos, small soldiers, want to kill the Gorgonites. But the ugly, friendly Gorgonites do not like fighting – they only want to go home. Can Alan Abernathy and his new friend Christy stop the Commandos? Or will the Commandos hurt them, and their families, too?

Gavin Scott was born in England in 1950. His parents moved to New Zealand when he was ten. He went to university in New Zealand. Later he moved back to England, and he began to write there. At first he worked for newspapers and television companies, but in 1990 he started to write for films. He worked on *The Young Indiana Jones Chronicles* and *The Borrowers*.

Scott is married and now lives in California with his wife, three daughters, and two cats. He writes for television and film, and he also writes books for young people.

Chapter 1 "They're only toys"

Irwin Wayfair was not a happy man. He made children's toys, and he always had a lot of new ideas. He liked children, and he loved his job. But today he had a new boss. Heartland Toys was suddenly a small and unimportant piece of a larger company – Globotech. Globotech made everything – guns, cars, trucks, computers, not only toys. The boss was Mr. Mars, a difficult man. Irwin had to meet him this morning, and he did not feel good about it.

Irwin met Larry Benson outside Mr. Mars's office. Larry made toys too, but the two men were not friends. Toys were Irwin's life. Larry was only interested in money.

"I think you two made this," said Mr. Mars.

"Good morning!" Mr. Mars walked past them into his office. "I'm Mr. Mars. I don't want to know your names. But from today, you work for me. I hope you're good at your jobs."

Irwin looked at Larry. Larry looked at the floor. They followed him into his office.

"I think you two made this," said Mr. Mars. He had a very ugly doll in his hand – a toy monster.

"Oh that," said Larry, quickly. "That was Irwin's idea."

Mars pushed the monster's stomach and it made a funny sound. The boss laughed happily. "Hey, I like that," he said.

"Oh, but I worked on the toy too," said Larry, "and now we sell a lot of them."

"Right," said Mars. "But I'm interested in the future. Show me your *new* ideas. Who's first?"

Irwin started. He took an ugly doll from his bag, and some pictures of other monsters. "These are the Gorgonites. This

"Oh that," said Larry, quickly. "That was Irwin's idea."

monster is Archer – he's their boss. The Gorgonites are from Gorgon and they want to go home. The children will help them, but they have to read about the world first. Then they can find the right home for the Gorgonites . . ."

"Stop," Mars shouted. "I hate it! Next?"

Larry had no pictures, no toys – only a video. The film showed a small toy soldier in a box. It could talk: "Chip Hazard, Commando," said the soldier to the camera. Then the soldier moved. It broke the box and climbed out.

"Hey, that's exciting," said Mars. "Can these toys really walk and talk?"

"No, Mr. Mars," said Larry, "that's only in the video. Commandos are only soldier dolls. But children will love them."

"They're great in the video," said Mars. "Now, listen to me. Globotech toys have to be the best. I want intelligent toys. Today, children play with toys. Tomorrow, toys will talk to children, and play with them too."

"That's interesting, but –" said Irwin.

"That's a great idea, Mr. Mars," said Larry quickly.

"But for toys like that, we'll have to use computer chips. We haven't got any," said Irwin.

"Oh, Irwin," said Larry, "we can find some."

"Yes," said Mars, "Globotech makes everything – we have chips. That's not a problem. You only have to ask. Now let me think." He looked out of the window. "The Commandos are soldiers and soldiers have to fight. It's their job. And children love fighting – they never stop. So who can the Commandos fight?"

Irwin was very unhappy now. "But Mr. Mars," he said, "it isn't good for children to play with fighting soldiers. What will parents think?"

Mars didn't listen to Irwin. "I know – they can fight those ugly Gorgonites. They're monsters. The Commandos have to find them – and kill them!"

Larry was excited now. "Yes, sir, Mr. Mars, sir. We can do that – the Commandos fight the Gorgonites and kill them! That's a great idea."

"I don't know," said Irwin slowly. "I don't like it."

"What's the problem?" asked Mars. "They're only toys."

Chapter 2   The Toy Store

In a small American town the school day ended, but Alan Abernathy could not go home. He got on his bicycle and went to work. He had to help his father.

Alan's dad, Stuart Abernathy, had a toy store. Parents liked the store. But there were no soldiers, no guns – only boats and balls and things. Most children thought the toys were boring.

That day, Alan's dad had to go away.

"Alan, you're late – where were you? I have to catch a plane – did you forget?" he said to his son.

"Dad, it's Friday. I was at school," said Alan.

"Oh, right. Now do everything on this piece of paper. Look at the store windows, and change some of the toys. Close the store carefully at the end of the day. And take the money home tonight – don't leave any in the store."

"Yes, Dad," said Alan.

"This is a big job for you, Alan." Stuart looked at his son. "You're the boss today. So be careful, and don't break anything!"

"OK, Dad," said Alan. "Have a good time."

"Goodbye, Alan."

Stuart drove home. He had to get his bag and say goodbye to his wife.

Now Alan was the boss. And he was bored. He walked round the store, but nobody came in. He put the radio on and listened to music. He read a magazine. Then he heard a noise outside.

It was Joe with his truck from Heartland Toys. Stuart Abernathy bought toys from Heartland every month. Alan liked Joe. They carried the new toys into the store.

Suddenly Alan saw some large boxes in the truck.

"Commandos? Gorgonites? What are those?"

"I don't know," answered Joe. "I think they're new. Let's have a look." Joe took two boxes into the store and opened the Commando box. Inside there was a toy soldier. He took the soldier out of the box, and stood it on the table.

"Good afternoon, sir!" said Joe, smiling at the toy.

Suddenly a small light on the toy began to shine. It stood up and moved a little. Then it answered Joe: "Chip Hazard, sir!"

Alan really liked the little soldier. He looked at the other box. "Archer the Gorgonite," he read. He opened the box carefully, and took out an ugly toy monster.

"Hello! I am Archer the Gorgonite," said the monster.

Alan laughed. "Joe, please can I have some of these?" he asked.

Joe thought for a minute. "Your dad didn't ask for them. He doesn't like guns – he never sells toy soldiers or weapons. He won't like these things."

Alan looked at the new toys again. He really wanted them. "Listen, Joe, my dad's not here," said Alan, "and I can make some money with these. I can sell them fast – please, Joe! You can have the money later."

"All right," said Joe. "I know this is a mistake, but . . . help me with the boxes."

So Alan and Joe brought the new toys into the store and put them down on the floor. Then Joe drove away. Alan now had six different soldiers and seven monsters.

He wanted to open the boxes, and put the new toys on the shelves – or in the store window. But two customers arrived. They were Christy Fimple, the prettiest girl in Alan's class, and her little brother Tim. Christy's house was behind Alan's, but he didn't know her very well.

"It's my birthday this week," said little Tim. "I'm here to look at the toys." Christy smiled at Alan and began to look round the store.

"I'm Alan Abernathy," said Alan. "We live in the house behind yours."

"I think I know your face," said Christy. "But I never see you after school."

"That's because I usually work here," said Alan.

They heard a noise from the back of the store: "We will win!" Then Tim ran to them. "Hey Christy, I want a soldier and a monster – listen, they can talk! And they can walk and fight. They're great!" Christy and Alan went with him to look at the Commandos and the Gorgonites.

"How much are they, Alan?" asked Christy.

"119 dollars," answered Alan.

"What!" said Christy. "I'm sorry, Tim – 119 dollars for a doll!

"119 dollars for a doll!"

6

Mom and Dad won't buy you those."

"Oh yes they will. You have dolls for *your* birthday."

"Not now – I'm sixteen," said Christy angrily. She had dolls in her room, but she didn't play with them. "Listen, Alan, can you put my name on one of the soldiers?"

"Yes, of course," answered Alan.

"And a monster," said Tim.

"No," said his sister. "Goodbye, Alan. Say hello sometimes."

After they left, Alan saw his father's tickets on the table. What time was it? He had to find his father quickly. He left the soldiers and monsters on the floor when he closed the store. It was a big mistake – but Alan didn't know that.

Chapter 3   Archer the Gorgonite

Alan took his schoolbag and went home on his bicycle. He went past Christy's house. Phil Fimple, Christy's dad, was in his yard. He liked big tools, big machines, and noise. There was a lot of noise now: Phil Fimple had to cut a tree down. He had a new satellite dish for his television, but the tree was in the way.

Alan's parents didn't really like Phil Fimple. Alan's dad liked quiet things; he liked beautiful toys. He made boats and dolls and little houses from wood for his store. He had all his tools there. Sometimes he sold the toys – sometimes.

Stuart Abernathy shouted at Phil Fimple: "Stop that noise!" But Phil Fimple shouted too: "I have to cut this tree down – is that a problem?"

Alan's dad was angry, but he had to leave. Then Alan ran into the house. "Hey, Dad, here are your plane tickets. You left them in the store," he called.

"Oh, thank you," said Stuart. "You're a good boy! Now, remember, you're the boss. Be careful in the store tomorrow –

"Hello. I am Archer the Gorgonite," said the monster.

don't break anything. And don't play with my tools!"

"OK, Dad." Alan went upstairs to his room.

He turned on his computer, then put his hand in his schoolbag. "What . . .? Something's moving in there!" he thought. He looked inside, and Archer the monster looked back at him. Alan took the toy out of his bag.

"Hello. I am Archer the Gorgonite," said the monster. "The fight will be long."

"Oh, really!" said Alan.

"I am Archer the Gorgonite," said the monster again. "What is your name?"

"I'm Alan, now be quiet," said Alan. "I have to do my school work."

"Hello, Alan-Now-Be-Quiet," said Archer.

"What!" said Alan. But now the monster was quiet.

Alan did his homework and ate his dinner. Then he listened to music. Later he turned off his computer, and went to bed. He left the toy monster on the table next to the computer. Alan was tired, and he went to sleep quickly.

Archer began to move again. He turned on the computer, and began to look at Microsoft *Encarta*. He found a beautiful picture of trees and flowers. "Home," said Archer quietly.

Alan woke up. "Strange," he thought, "the computer is on." Then he saw Archer in front of the computer.

"What are you?" asked Alan suddenly. "You're very different from other toys. Talk to me."

Archer turned round quickly. "Hello, Alan-Now-Be-Quiet!" he said. "I am Archer the Gorgonite."

"I think you're really smart," said Alan. "Listen – my name's Alan, OK?"

"Hello, Alan," said Archer.

"Now – walk to the end of my table," said Alan. Archer thought for a minute, then walked to the end of the table.

"Alan, friend of Archer," he said, "friend of the Gorgonites. You have to help us." Alan looked at him. He didn't understand. "This toy can talk and walk," he thought. "And it can turn on a computer."

"The fight will be long," said Archer.

"OK. Say something different now," said Alan.

"The fight will be long," said Archer.

"I don't think you are very smart," said Alan. He put Archer in his bag. Then he closed the bag carefully.

"Tomorrow," Alan thought, "he's going back to the toy store."

Chapter 4   "The Gorgonites will die!"

That same night, in the toy store, Chip Hazard climbed out of his box. He stood up. "Commandos! Here! Now!" he shouted. Five

9

"You are the Commandos. Your job — to kill the Gorgonites."

more small soldiers climbed out of their boxes. They stood in front of Chip Hazard. "Men, are you all here?" asked Chip. "Give me your names."

The first soldier answered: "Link Static, sir! I work on radios."

Then the other soldiers spoke.

"Brick Bazooka. The greatest soldier. I love guns."

"Kip Killigan, sir. I can hide anywhere."

"Butch Meathook, sir. Good with a gun. I can hit anything."

"Nick Nitro. Explosions. The biggest explosions! I'm ready, sir!"

Five small soldiers — six with Chip Hazard.

Chip Hazard spoke to his soldiers. "Right, men. You are the Commandos. Your job — to kill the Gorgonites. The Gorgonites will die!"

"Yes, sir," shouted the five small soldiers.

Chip broke his little toy gun in two pieces.

"But first, men, find some good weapons," he said.

"Yes, sir!" the five answered.

They saw Stuart Abernathy's tools, and moved fast. Only a few minutes later, the small soldiers had new weapons – Stuart's best tools.

Now Chip spoke to his men again. "Commandos! We will fight the Gorgonites, and we will win! Find the Gorgonites," he shouted, "and kill them all!"

Chapter 5   A Difficult Saturday

The next day was Saturday. Alan looked in his bag. Good – Archer the Gorgonite was there. Alan got on his bicycle and went to the toy store. He opened the door, turned on the light – "Oh no!" There were toys on the floor, in pieces. And where were his father's best tools? They were not on the shelf.

Archer climbed out of Alan's bag, but Alan didn't see him. His eyes were on the Commando boxes. There were no toy soldiers in them now. He turned round and saw Archer. "Who did this?" he asked. Archer looked at the Commando boxes, then looked at Alan.

"What – the toy soldiers? Those stupid Commandos? No!"

"The Commandos have to kill the Gorgonites," said Archer.

"Well, I know one thing," said Alan, "*I* didn't do this. I know – I'll speak to Globotech. There's a big problem with these ... things!"

He called Globotech, but a computer answered the phone. "This is Globotech," said the machine. "For Globotech Guns, push 1. For Globotech Trucks, push 2. For Globotech Computers, push 3. For Heartland Toys, push 4." Alan pushed number 4 and waited to speak to somebody. But it was another machine: "Everybody at Heartland Toys is busy. Please wait. Have you got our new Commandos – the toys that play with children?" Alan put the phone down angrily.

There was somebody at the door. "Sorry, the store's closed," he shouted. "Oh, Christy, it's you."

"I only want to buy a soldier and a monster," said Christy.

"Sorry, I can't sell them. There's a problem."

Suddenly Christy saw the toys in pieces on the floor. "What happened here? Hey, Alan, do you want some help?"

"Yes, please!"

Christy and Alan worked hard, and four hours later the store was fine again. Christy was busy with the last toy, a beautiful boat. Alan talked to Christy about his past. He was a bad boy when he was young, but these days he tried to be good – sometimes. Christy was interested. Then he asked about her.

"Everybody thinks I'm always happy. But I'm not," she said. "Sometimes I'm sad or angry. Nobody understands me."

"*I* understand," said Alan.

"Really?" Christy looked at him. Now they were good friends.

But then Alan's dad walked in. "Hello," he said. Then his mouth fell open. "What happened in here? Look at this boat – look at it!"

"I'm going," said Christy. She saw Archer and the two pieces of a toy monster on the floor. She quickly put them in her bag and left.

"You go too, Alan," Stuart said angrily.

Outside, Christy gave Archer and Troglokhan, the other monster, to Alan. "Here, have your toys back," she said. Her boyfriend, Brad, was there too, with his new car. He laughed at Alan – toys! Alan felt angry. "Christy thinks I'm stupid now," he thought. "And those toys – are they toys? I'll have to call Globotech again."

Alan put Archer in his bag. He looked at the pieces of Troglokhan and threw them away. Then he got on his bicycle and started for home. A small soldier watched him. It was Link Static. He saw Alan on his bicycle, then told the other soldiers by radio, "Alan is going home. He's leaving now."

"Ready, men? Wait — can you see him?"

Chip Hazard and the other small soldiers waited at the other
end of the road. Chip spoke quietly. "Ready, men? Brick Bazooka
— are you ready to fight? Wait — can you see him? Now!" Brick
Bazooka ran to Alan's bicycle, and jumped on.

Alan felt nothing. He moved fast and turned into his street.
Suddenly the soldier was on the ground — in two pieces. But he
could talk through his radio.

"I can see the boy's house," said Brick Bazooka. "And Archer
the Gorgonite is with the boy."

"Brick — we're coming," answered Chip Hazard. "Wait, my man!"

◆

At home Alan tried to call Globotech again. This time, he got a
person. "What is the name of the toy and what is the problem?"
she asked.

"The Commandos and the Gorgonites," answered Alan. "They
broke everything in my father's store, and they ran away."

Alan felt nothing. He moved fast and turned into his street.

"I'm sorry," said the woman at Heartland Toys. "You lost the toys – it's your problem, not ours. We can't help you."

"But there's a big problem," said Alan. "The toys are dangerous! They fight, they break things. I can't stop them because I can't turn them off!"

"Yeah, yeah, OK," said the woman. "It's only a boy," she thought. Alan put the phone down angrily. He looked at Archer. "Don't talk to me!" he said. Then he sat down and listened to loud music.

The woman at Globotech told Irwin and Larry about Alan's telephone call. Irwin was afraid. But Larry did not think there was a problem.

"These toys aren't dangerous," said Larry. "They're only toys."

"But perhaps the boy's right. We can't sell dangerous toys," said Irwin. He turned on his computer and looked at the plans for the Commandos and Gorgonites. He read quietly. Then he looked up. "Where are the computer chips from?" he asked.

"Oh, they were for weapons – very expensive. Why?"

"You put chips for weapons into toys?" shouted Irwin. "I think that's the problem. We have to do something about it now."

Larry looked at Irwin. "I think perhaps you're right this time," he said slowly. "Tomorrow, we'll go to Globotech Guns. We'll talk to the people there."

Chapter 6   Problems for Archer

That night Alan went to bed early. Of course, Archer did not sleep – he was a toy. He sat and thought on Alan's table. Then he heard a funny noise. "Help!" said something – or somebody. "A Gorgonite – they're not all dead!" thought Archer. He went downstairs. "Help!" he heard. The noise came from a closet!

Archer opened the closet, and looked inside. "Kill the Gorgonites!" shouted Chip Hazard. Butch Meathook and Nick Nitro jumped on Archer and carried him away.

A minute later Archer was in the kitchen. His feet were above his head, and his head was over a dangerous machine. "This is the end for you, Gorgonite!" said Chip Hazard. "Now talk! Where are the other Gorgonites?"

Archer suddenly felt happy inside – the other Gorgonites weren't dead! But he said nothing.

"Right. Let's turn the machine on!" said Chip. Archer closed his eyes.

But then Alan arrived and turned on the light. "Hey!" he shouted. The three Commandos ran; Alan took Archer out of the

His feet were above his head, and his head was over a dangerous machine.

machine. Chip Hazard and Butch Meathook quickly climbed through the window. But Nick Nitro stayed in the kitchen, and he had a knife. He stood on the table behind Alan, then pushed the knife hard into Alan's arm. "Ooow!" shouted Alan. He turned round, and took the soldier in his hand. Then he pushed him hard into the machine and turned it on. There was a loud noise, and the machine stopped. The soldier was in pieces.

Alan's parents ran into the kitchen. "What's all this noise? What's happening?" shouted Stuart.

"Alan, your arm!" said his mother, Irene.

Alan told them about the soldiers. "You were away, Dad, and Joe came. He had these soldiers, and he gave me some. I wanted to sell them – I wanted to make money. I know it was wrong. I really am very, very sorry."

Stuart looked at Irene. "Really?" he said to his son. "So, did you sell my tools? Did you pay Joe with money from my tools?"

"No, Dad, I think the toy soldiers took the tools."

"Alan – do you think I'm stupid?"

Alan looked at Archer. "Archer – help me – say something!" Nothing.

His mother looked at him. "Alan, go to bed, dear," she said quietly. "And wash that cut on your arm."

They all left the kitchen. Nobody saw Nick Nitro climb slowly through the open window with one leg under his arm.

Chapter 7   "Where can a Gorgonite hide?"

It was dark in Phil Fimple's garage, but the small soldiers were all there.

"Men – Commandos – come here!" shouted Chip Hazard. "Now we know the Gorgonites' friend. He is big. He is fast.

17

Now they could make new weapons – fighting machines, trucks, everything!

Things are different now." He looked at Link Static. The soldier turned on the light in the garage.

There were tools there. Now they could make new weapons – fighting machines, trucks, everything!

Nick Nitro arrived. "Doctor!" he called. Chip Hazard ran to him.

"It's bad, Chip," said Nick.

"You did a good job," said Chip quietly.

"Did we win?" asked Nick.

"We *will* win," answered Chip.

Nick smiled at Chip Hazard – then his eyes closed and his light went off.

Chip Hazard stood up and spoke to his men. "We will win! We have to make weapons – we have to make trucks – we have to make guns – we have to make fighting machines. Use these tools – use everything – move! Fast! Kill all Gorgonites! The Gorgonites will die!"

But that was in the Fimple garage. In Alan's house it was quiet. Alan wanted to talk to Archer, but Archer didn't answer. This made Alan angry. "I know – I can throw the Gorgonites away. My dad thinks I'm crazy. Christy thinks I'm stupid. And Joe – well . . ."

Archer looked at Alan. "The Gorgonites aren't dead," he said.

"What?" said Alan.

"Chip Hazard is looking for the Gorgonites," answered Archer.

"OK – I understand," said Alan. "He's looking for them, so they have to *be* somewhere. But where *are* they?"

"My Gorgonites are hiding – they do that very well."

♦

Next morning was Sunday, so it was very quiet. The toy store didn't open on Sundays, but Alan was there. He looked for the Gorgonites but he couldn't find them. "Why are they hiding?" he asked Archer. "They're monsters – can't they fight the Commandos?"

"No, Alan, we always lose," said Archer. "It's in the computer chips."

"Hide or lose? That's sad," said Alan. Then he looked at a Gorgonite box. "On the box it says you're looking for home. Did they go to find their home?"

"Not without me," said Archer, "I'm their boss."

Alan thought: "Where can a Gorgonite hide? They fight but they never win. They always lose, they hide. They are sad – I know!" He ran outside and looked behind the store. There were boxes and old toys there. Archer followed him and looked too. It was a good place to hide.

· "Hey, you in there – you can come out! I'm a friend!" Nothing. Alan turned back to the store.

"Ocula," shouted Archer. Alan turned again, and saw a big eye with legs! Something moved, and there were the small toy monsters. Archer said hello to each one. "Punch-It! Scratch-It! Insaniac! Slamfist! Troglokhan – what did they do to you?" They were all very ugly, but Troglokhan was the ugliest.

"We connected his head, and the pieces of his arms and legs, to an old radio," laughed Punch-It.

"So, you're all here. I can give you back to Joe." Alan found a large box on the ground. "Perhaps things are getting better," he thought. "OK, everybody in!" he said. Then he took the Gorgonites home.

Chapter 8   Problems with Chips

That same Sunday morning, Larry and Irwin were at Globotech Guns. They walked into an office.

"Who are you?" said a man. "No visitors in here!"

Larry spoke. "Listen, it's me — Larry. You gave me some computer chips for toys."

"Oh, I remember," said the man, "They're great chips."

"Yes — thank you," answered Larry. "But there's a problem."

"There's no problem with my computer chips," said the man angrily. "The problem is your toys. The computer chips are fine — they're intelligent, they can learn."

Larry and Irwin looked at him.

"Yes, my friends, they can learn," he said. "These computer chips are really very, very good. But there's one little problem, so nobody wants them."

"So there *is* a problem then?" asked Irwin quickly.

"Yes," said the man. "When there's a very strong electromagnetic field, the computer chips don't work. That's the end of them. It's a great problem for weapons, but not for toys!"

Larry and Irwin left the office. "Let's tell Mr. Mars that there's a problem."

"We can't do that!" said Larry. He didn't want to lose his job.

"Well, then, we have to go and find those toys," said Irwin. "That boy doesn't want them."

"Yes, I think you're right."

"And we'll tell Joe to get the toys from the other stores. They can't sell them – the toys are dangerous."

"OK, Irwin," said Larry. "Now, let's go and see this Alan Abernathy."

♦

In Alan's bedroom Gorgonites were everywhere. Troglokhan used the computer. Ocula and Slamfist watched television. Punch-It sat and thought. Scratch-It jumped up and down on the bed. Insaniac played happily with the family cat. "What am I going to do with you?" said Alan. But then he heard his mother.

"Alan!" she called.

"Gorgonites – hide now!" said Archer. And they hid!

Alan's mother opened the door and came in. "Christy called," she said. "Here's her number." She gave Alan a piece of paper with the number on it and left.

"What is Christy?" asked the Gorgonites.

"Not what – who!" said Alan. "She's a girl. I really like her. Why did she call?"

"Ask her!" said the Gorgonites.

"But I'm a little – well, afraid," said Alan slowly.

"Afraid!" shouted the Gorgonites. "Then you have to hide. She will hurt you!"

"No," said Alan, "I really like her – she's great."

"You aren't afraid?" asked Archer.

"Well, no."

"Then call her!" said Archer. Alan looked at him – he was right. So Alan called Christy.

"Oh, hello, Alan," she said. "Was your dad really angry about the store?"

"No – not really." Alan thought hard. "Would you like to come to the movies with me, Christy?" he asked.

"Alan, I have a boyfriend. I'm going out with Brad. He's older than you. And my mother doesn't like you. People tell her things . . ."

21

"Well, I don't want you to have problems with your mom because of me."

"OK. Goodbye, Alan," said Christy.

"Goodbye," said Alan, and he put the phone down sadly. He looked at the monsters. "Thank you for your help," he said. "Why do I listen to toys?"

In the garage, Commando Link Static put his radio down and went to Chip Hazard.

"I connected my radio to their telephones. I heard them, sir," he said. "The boy likes the girl."

"Good – we are learning," said Chip Hazard. "The boy is weak. He likes girls. We have to do something now – the time is right! Go, men, go!"

Chapter 9   Commandos 3: Fimples 0

In Christy's house, her mother and father were in the living-room. The new satellite dish was in place, and the television was on.

"That's a great picture," said Marion Fimple. She brought two drinks and put them on the table.

Brad arrived. Christy came down from her room and said goodbye to her parents. "Don't wait for me. I'll be back late, so you go to bed." Then she and Brad left in his fast new car.

The Fimples sat in the dark and watched television – and three small soldiers watched the Fimples. Chip Hazard saw the drinks on the table.

"To the bathroom, men!" he said. "They have to sleep!" Upstairs, the three Commandos looked in the bathroom closet. They found sleeping pills. Then they went downstairs again, with the bottle of pills.

Chip opened the bottle and Kip Killigan put a pill in his gun.

Go! The pill went very high and then it fell on the floor. Next time Butch Meathook helped, and the pill fell into one of the glasses. A minute later there were two pills in each glass. And two minutes after that, Phil and Marion Fimple were asleep. Commandos 2: Fimples 0.

"Good, men!" said Chip Hazard. "Now – the girl's room!"

Chip and the two other soldiers ran through Christy's bedroom door. At the same time, Brick Bazooka and Link Static came through the window. They shouted "AAAAAAAAAAAhhh," but then stopped. There was nobody there – only Commandos.

"She is not in here," said Chip. "Look everywhere." But suddenly somebody turned the light on. It was Tim. He came into the room, the happiest boy in town.

"Great!" he said. "Five small soldiers – five Commandos – for my birthday!" He looked at the toys.

"Stop, men," said Chip Hazard. Chip wanted to think.

"Hey, great," said Tim. "You can talk." He sat down on the floor and began to play. "You're Chip," he said, "and you're the boss." Then he took Kip Killigan in his hand. "Kip fights you one day, and he wins. So now he's the boss."

Chip was not happy. "This is stupid," he thought. Then he shouted, "Men! Fight him!" The soldiers ran at Tim, but he only laughed happily. Tim was stronger and bigger than the toys, so he won the fight easily. The soldiers ran away and hid.

But Tim wanted to play again. "All right," he said. "Now you can win – and I'll lose, OK?" Suddenly the Commandos were on him. Tim's arms were behind him and there was something round them. He couldn't move his hands. "That hurts!" he shouted. "I can't move! This isn't funny! Hey!" But Chip put something in his mouth, and other soldiers worked on his legs. Then they pushed him into Christy's closet.

Commandos 3: Fimples 0.

"Good work, men!" said Chip. The soldiers stopped and

looked round the room. On a shelf there were a lot of beautiful dolls.

"Well, hello!" said Kip. "Girls!"

Chip looked up. "We can use these young women. They can fight with us. Now, where is Nick Nitro?" Two soldiers brought the dead Commando. Chip Hazard broke the toy's head. And then he took out the intelligent computer chip. "Men – to work. Bring the dolls."

Two hours later, the dolls looked very different. They had no hair. In their heads were small computer chips – from old phones and other machines from Phil Fimple's garage. The dolls were all on the floor, with Tim's electric train. The intelligent computer chip from Nick Nitro's head was now in the train. Link Static connected the dolls to the train.

"Let's finish now," said Chip. "Is the train ready? And the chip? Right – let's connect the dolls to the electricity."

Slowly the dolls all stood up. "Hi, boys!" said one. The girl dolls were not toys now – they were soldiers.

"Strange soldiers," thought Chip. "But they can fight with us. Now we are stronger!"

Chapter 10   "Gorgonites, you can't win!"

When Christy and Brad came home, it was very late. Phil and Marion Fimple were asleep in the living-room.

"Goodnight, Brad," said Christy. She was tired. She went up to her room, and put her coat away in the closet. It was dark, so she did not see Tim in there. And Tim couldn't speak, because there was something in his mouth.

She put on the light in her room but nothing happened. She tried a different light. Then the door closed suddenly with a loud noise. Something ran under the bed. And then Christy saw the

*The dolls all looked at Christy. The pretty faces were ugly now –
and they had no hair.*

dolls. One doll opened its eyes and sat up. "I'm beautiful.
Everybody likes me," it said. The dolls all looked at Christy. The
pretty faces were ugly now – and they had no hair.

Christy shouted loudly – and outside, Brad heard the noise.
He got out of his car and ran into the house: "Christy – it's all
right! I'm coming!" He ran upstairs and into Christy's room –
and stopped. Christy was on the floor and she couldn't move or
speak. Round her stood these ugly dolls. "What the . . ." Brad
began, and then a doll jumped on him.

"You're pretty!" said the doll. A second doll arrived. "Take me
to the movies!" she said. Then the others began to fight Brad.
They hit him and pulled his hair. They climbed up his legs and
ran up his arms. He fought back hard. "No! No!" he shouted. He
moved to the door – but the Commandos were in his way.

"Men do not fight women," said Chip Hazard. Brad stopped
and looked at the small soldiers. He looked at the ugly dolls. He

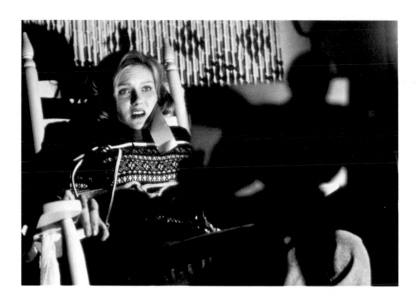

"Are you afraid?" Chip asked her.

looked at Christy on the floor. This time, he did not say goodbye – he ran downstairs and out of the house. Then he jumped into his car and drove away fast.

Upstairs, the Commandos went into Christy's room with Phil Fimple's video camera.

"Are you afraid?" Chip asked her.

Christy was not afraid – she was very, very afraid.

♦

It was very late, but Alan and the Gorgonites were not asleep. Ocula looked out of Alan's window and made a strange noise. Alan looked up. "What can you see?" he asked. Then the window broke – and a video flew into the room. There were some words on the video box: *You can't win!* Alan put the video into his machine, and began to watch. He saw Christy, with papers in her hand. She read from them slowly.

"I am fine. The Commandos didn't hurt me. They always win because they are the best fighters. Ooh, there are pages and pages of this. Ouch!" She looked away from the camera. "I'm doing it, I'm reading it," she said. She looked at the camera again. "I can leave this room, but first two things have to happen. One, you have to give the ugly Gorgonites to the Commandos. Gorgonites, you can't win! Two – er – that's all. Alan, please ..." And then the picture went. Alan was very angry. And the Gorgonites were afraid.

"So, Chip Hazard wants to fight. Then we will fight!" shouted Alan.

Archer spoke. "No, Alan. We have to lose. We can't fight. It's in our computer chips."

Alan looked at Archer. "Forget the computer chips. The Commandos are only stupid toys, and you *can* win. Come with me!"

A few minutes later there was a box outside the Fimples' house, and on the box was the word *Gorgonites*. From the box came noises: "We're afraid!"; "Alan – don't do this!"; "Help!"; "No!" The sounds of the Gorgonite monsters.

Inside the Fimples' house, the Commandos watched and listened. They had new weapons, new trucks, and fighting machines. Now there was nothing in Mr. Fimple's garage, and there were no machines in the Fimples' kitchen. The Commandos had everything.

"The door!" Chip Hazard said. "Careful, men! Let's go!"

Alan and Archer were in the Fimples' yard. "You *can* fight!" said Alan quietly. "The rocket is ready; you'll be OK. Five ... four ... three ... two ... one ... go, go, go!" Archer flew on the toy rocket, up and up. Then he came down, through an open window, into the house.

He stood up and opened the back door for Alan. Alan put Archer in his bag and walked quietly upstairs. He opened Christy's bedroom door.

"Five ... four ... three ... two ... one ... go, go, go!"

"You'll be OK now, Christy," he said. He ran to her.

"Be careful! Behind you!" shouted Christy. The soldier girl dolls jumped on Alan with knives and other small weapons. Alan turned round and fell. But Christy jumped up and hit the dolls hard. They flew across the room and broke into pieces.

"Christy? Are you OK?" said Alan.

She smiled at him. "Thank you, Alan – you came for me! Let's move, and get those Commandos!"

Outside the house, the Commandos stood round the box and listened to the Gorgonites. Brick Bazooka opened the box a little, and put something inside. The Commandos all smiled – this was the end of the Gorgonites! There was a small explosion. Then the Commandos looked in the box, but there were no Gorgonites. Only an answer machine. Now the Commandos were really angry.

Chapter 11 "Old soldiers never die"

Alan and Christy went downstairs slowly, but the Commandos saw them. So they ran upstairs again to Christy's window.

"It's OK, it's not high here," she said. "Jump!" Then they were in the yard.

Suddenly there was a loud explosion, and the garage door broke.

Christy and Alan tried to get up quickly. There was a lot of smoke. Then small machines drove out of the garage. "You can't win!" shouted Chip. But Christy had a bicycle. Alan sat behind her and Archer was in his bag.

"Are you all right, Alan?" she asked. "Did we lose the Commandos?"

"I don't know – let's find help."

They went past some tall trees. Suddenly there was an explosion, and a tree fell down. Christy moved fast and did not hit it. But then Archer looked behind them.

The Commandos were there in three small trucks. Archer watched. The machines were closer, then they connected. Suddenly there was one larger machine, not three smaller ones. It moved faster than Christy's bicycle.

"Alan," said Archer. Alan looked round too.

"What! It's bigger! How did that happen?"

Then there was another explosion. Christy had no time to stop. "Down, Alan!" she shouted, but the tree hit him. He fell off the bicycle. Christy stopped and he ran to her. He got on again. Then another tree fell down in front of them. They couldn't move.

"Oh no," said Christy. Then, "Look!" To the left there was a small river. "We can jump it – I'll go really fast!"

"Be careful, Christy!" shouted Alan. The bicycle went faster and faster. Then they flew over the river and hit the ground hard. But they were all OK.

The Commandos' big machine arrived at the river with a loud noise. It flew up, then hit the ground very hard. There was a very loud explosion. The machine broke, the Commandos broke, and the pieces fell into the river. It was the end of the Commandos.

Or was it? Chip Hazard was in the water and he was in one piece. Alan, Christy, and Archer looked at the moving water and saw the pieces of toy soldiers. But they didn't see Chip Hazard.

"I think that's the end of the fight," said Alan. "Can we go now?"

"Yes, please, let's go home!" said Archer. Christy laughed.

Alan was on the front of the bicycle now. Christy sat behind him – and Archer sat behind Christy. He didn't want to hide in the bag. "We won!" he thought. "That was the end of the Commandos!"

But it was not the end – it was the start of a long fight. Chip carefully climbed out of the water. "Old soldiers never die," he said slowly. Then he stood up. He felt strong again. "We lost a small fight. But the Commandos will win the big fight. We will not lose! We cannot lose!"

When Alan, Christy, and Archer got home, there were four angry parents in Alan's yard. Little Tim was there too. They all went into Alan's house.

"Alan, where were you?" asked his father.

"Christy, are you all right? Did that boy hurt you?" asked Christy's father.

"Wait – let's wait a minute. First, what happened?" asked Alan's mother.

Phil Fimple started. "Your son took my daughter. He ran away with her, and her bicycle. And he put something in our drinks too! Marion feels sick!"

"I'm fine now, Phil," Marion said. But she was very tired.

"And my house and my garage?" said Phil Fimple angrily. "And those explosions?"

"Don't forget those monsters, dear," said Marion Fimple. The Gorgonites tried to hide behind the flowers.

"They talked to us!" said Stuart.

"I'm sorry – we're sorry," said the Gorgonites.

Chapter 12   Dangerous Times

Joe drove from store to store in his truck. He had to get every Commando and Gorgonite, and take them back to Globotech. He didn't understand – but he did it. He was a good worker.

Then suddenly he understood. There was a small soldier on his arm – and a knife in front of his eye!

"You are with us now," said Chip Hazard. "Drive to Alan Abernathy's house. Move! Fast! Faster!"

◆

Alan and Christy told their parents the story of the Commandos and the Gorgonites. Then they stopped and looked at them.

"I think it really happened," said Alan's dad.

"Me too," said his mom.

"Are you all crazy?" shouted Christy's dad. "Christy, Tim, Marion, let's go." He opened the door – but there was somebody outside.

"Hello," said Irwin. "I'm Irwin Wayfair from Heartland Toys, and this is Larry Benson. We're looking for Alan Abernathy. He called us. Is there a problem with some of our toys?"

"There was a problem with the Commandos," said Alan.

"Really?" said Larry. "What problem? That isn't possible."

Stuart thought about his store and Phil Fimple's garage, and he suddenly got angry. He hit Larry hard and Larry fell to the floor. "Stuart!" shouted Irene. "Hit him again!"

The Gorgonites watched all this. Larry stood up, but he said

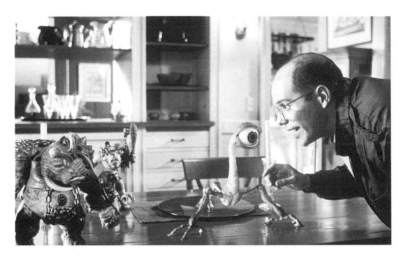

"I'm Irwin. I made you," said Irwin, excited. "And the other Gorgonites."

nothing. Then Irwin saw Archer. "Look, Larry," he said, "it's Archer!"

"Hello, I am Archer," said Archer. "Who are you?"

"I'm Irwin. I made you," said Irwin, excited. "And the other Gorgonites. You're all here – you can talk – you can move! Larry, they're great!"

Suddenly the lights went off. Alan looked out the window. "Oh no!" he said.

"What? Is it the Commandos again?" asked Christy.

"Yes, and this time there are hundreds of them," answered Alan. Joe's truck was outside, and the small soldiers came out, ten at a time. Joe was inside but he couldn't move.

Chip Hazard arrived in his fighting machine. Phil Fimple opened the door. "Hi, soldier," he said. "You win – let's talk about it."

"You can't stop now!" shouted Chip. "You have to fight! All Gorgonites will die!" A ball of fire flew at the house. Phil ran inside. "What did I do?" he asked.

Larry answered. "They're fighting everybody."

"We aren't Commandos," said Irwin, "so I think we have to be Gorgonites."

The Commandos began to fight. They had trucks with guns, fighting machines, knives. It was dangerous out there.

The window broke. Then a big fighting machine sent tennis balls on fire through the window into the house. Irene pushed Marion and Tim into a closet. Then she started to hit the tennis balls outside. The balls came down on the Commandos. Some soldiers fell, but then they stood up again.

"How can we stop them?" shouted Stuart. "Irene is good at tennis, but she can't do everything!"

"An electric field – a strong electromagnetic field," said Irwin. "That's the only answer."

"Then let's make one," shouted Christy.

Then a big fighting machine sent tennis balls on fire through the window into the house.

"Hah! Do you think it's easy?" said Larry.

Then Phil Fimple spoke: "Every electric machine makes an electromagnetic field." Something hit the windows. The Commandos were very near the house now.

"We want a big one," said Alan. Perhaps Phil Fimple was not a bad man really. He knew a lot about machines and electricity.

"They're in the back yard," shouted Alan. Suddenly he had an idea. "Look – outside. Can you see? Up there, there are two transformers. Can we use them to make an electromagnetic thing?"

"Electromagnetic field," said Irwin. "We'll have to make an explosion."

Phil Fimple spoke again, and everybody listened. "We have to connect the transformers with a big piece of metal. The electricity will go through the metal, and there's your explosion. The electromagnetic field will follow."

Alan began to move fast. He went into the kitchen and found a heavy metal tool. "This will connect the two transformers," he thought. Then his father came in. "Alan, what are you thinking? You can't go outside. It's dangerous."

"Have you got a better idea?" asked Alan.

"You're my son, and you can't . . ."

Alan looked at him. "Dad, I have to do this."

Stuart looked at his son. Did he know this young man? "Let's go, Alan," he said.

Archer watched them leave, then he hid in a closet.

Chapter 13 The Last Big Fight

Outside, there were Commandos everywhere. Stuart fought hard. They were only small soldiers, but they never stopped. Their weapons were small, but they were dangerous. Alan ran to the posts with the two transformers. He had to get there quickly and climb up, but the Commandos tried to stop him.

Christy, Irwin, and Larry were now in Christy's house, but it was dangerous there too. The Commandos wanted to get inside.

In Alan's kitchen, the Gorgonites stopped hiding. "Gorgonites – we have to help Alan," said Archer.

"We can't fight – we'll lose," said Slamfist.

"But we can't hide – we'll lose," answered Archer. "Let's fight!" he shouted.

"Yes!" shouted the others. So they ran outside.

They fought hard and well. The Commandos began to fight with the Gorgonites now, so Alan's job was easier. He climbed up one of the posts, and he was ready to connect the transformers. But then Chip Hazard arrived. This time he was in a small flying machine, like a little plane. There were two rockets, then an explosion, and Alan's metal tool fell from his hands. Chip came nearer. "Oh no!" thought Alan. "This is the end! I'm going to fall."

Now Chip brought the plane to the ground and climbed up

This time he was in a small flying machine, like a little plane.

to Alan. He had a knife. But Archer arrived and the two toys fought. "The Gorgonites will die!" shouted Chip, and Archer fell to the ground. Chip was now very near Alan, so Alan put out his hand: "That's it, you stupid toy," he said. "I haven't got that metal tool, so I can use you." He took Chip in his hand, and pushed him hard between the two transformers.

Then he jumped down to the ground. Christy was there. "Come into the house!" she shouted.

The metal inside Chip Hazard connected the two transformers. Electricity ran through him. Slowly the toy changed. Now you could only see the metal inside the toy: it was hot and white. Then the electromagnetic field started, and there was a loud explosion.

And in each small soldier there was a small explosion. They all fell down. Heads turned or fell off. Arms and legs moved fast, then slowly. Then they all stopped.

Christy and Alan were inside again. Stuart threw his arms round them – all four parents were very happy. And Larry put his arm round Irwin. But where were the Gorgonites?

Chapter 14   "Thank you, satellite dish"

An hour later, a small plane arrived in the street and Mr. Mars climbed out. First he saw Joe and his truck. "You work for us, don't you? That's a Globotech truck. I don't want to read this story in the newspapers. Drive that truck away!"

Joe looked at him. "I can't drive very well," he said. "My head hurts."

Mr. Mars gave Joe some money. "Here, you can put this in the bank," said Mars.

Joe looked at the money. "I feel better. I'll go now, Mr. Mars," he said. He started the truck and drove away.

Next it was Phil Fimple. "Look at my house and garage! And

my television, my tools, my new satellite dish." Mr. Mars took out some more money. Phil Fimple looked at it and was quiet.

"And our house?" asked Irene.

"And the problems?" said Stuart. Mr. Mars looked at him, then gave him some money too.

Last, Larry and Irwin. Now they were friends. Larry spoke. "It was my idea to use the computer chips, Mr. Mars," he said. "I'm sorry."

"Oh?" said Mars. "You made a big mistake. Now – how much did these toys cost in the stores?"

"119 dollars," answered Larry.

"Very cheap! Make them expensive," said Mars. "We'll sell them to South American fighters. Now get in the plane."

The plane flew away into the night.

Little Tim Fimple was half asleep. "Dad, you know my birthday," he said, "I only want clothes this year."

The Fimples went home. Alan's parents went in too, but Alan stayed outside. He wanted to look for the Gorgonites.

He looked everywhere for Archer and the others, but he could not find them. Christy came out again for a minute.

"Did you find Archer?" she asked.

"No," he answered sadly.

"I have to go," said Christy. "See you later?"

Alan looked at her. "She wants to see me again," he thought. "Yes, OK," he said, quietly.

He began to clean the yard. He threw the dead Commandos into a bag.

Suddenly he heard a noise. It came from the satellite dish. The dish was on the ground in his yard. He looked under it and found the Gorgonites. But they did not look good.

"Archer – are you OK?" he shouted.

"Hello, I am Archer the Gorgonite," said Archer slowly.

"Oh no – the electromagnetic field hit your computer chip

"Gorgonites are good at hiding. So we hid."

too," said Alan sadly. "But the Commandos are all dead."

"The Commandos are dead?" Archer asked. He turned to the others. "Gorgonites! We won!" Suddenly the Gorgonites moved again. They laughed and ran round the yard.

"Archer, I'm so happy – you're all OK!" laughed Alan.

"Of course we're OK," said Archer, "Gorgonites are good at hiding. So we hid. Thank you, Mr. Fimple – thank you, satellite dish."

◆

It was a sunny day. Alan was next to the river with one of Stuart's beautiful toy boats. And on the boat were the Gorgonites.

"Do you really want to go?" asked Alan.

"Yes, Alan, it's time," answered Archer.

"I understand. But where are you going?"

"Home. To Gorgon."

"But Archer, there is no . . ."

"Alan, we have to *look* for our country."

Alan stood up and pushed the boat into the water. The river carried it away.

"Goodbye, Alan!" they shouted. He stood and watched. The boat moved slowly away.

"Goodbye my friends," Alan said quietly.

Then there was nothing.

ACTIVITIES

Chapters 1–5

Before you read

1 Some children have jobs, or they help their parents after school. Is that a good idea?

2 Find these words in your dictionary. They are all in the story.

computer chip   doll   explosion   hide   machine   monster piece   satellite dish   soldier   tool   toy   truck   weapon

a Put these words in the table below:

doll   gun   camera   video   knife   ball

What other words can you put in the table?

Toys	Weapons	Machines

b Is a computer chip big or small?

c Is an explosion loud or quiet?

d Why do some animals hide in the day?

e Do you think there are monsters in the ocean?

f When you cut a cake in half, how many pieces are there?

g Why do people buy satellite dishes?

h What tools does a student of English use?

i Would you like to be a soldier? Why/why not?

j Would you like to be a truck driver? Why/why not?

After you read

3 How are the Commandos and the Gorgonites different from other toys?

4 Who are these people? What do you know about them?

   a Larry Benson   **d** Alan Abernathy

   b Irwin Wayfair   **e** Brad

   c Phil Fimple   **f** Stuart Abernathy

Chapters 6–10

Before you read

5 Why are Irwin and Larry going to visit Globotech Guns?

6 Find these words in your dictionary. Answer the questions about them.

connect   electric/electricity   electromagnetic field   pill   rocket

   a How is life at home different without electricity?

   b What happens when you connect a light to electricity?

   c What makes an electromagnetic field?

   d Why do people take pills?

   e Would you like to go on a rocket? Where to?

After you read

7 Tim Fimple tries to play with the Commandos. Why is this a bad idea?

8 How do the Gorgonites change in these chapters?

9 Work with another student.

   Student A: You are Christy. Talk to Alan. How do you feel about him now?

   Student B: You are Alan. Talk to Christy. How do you feel about her? Why?

Chapters 11–14

Before you read

10 What do you think the Commandos will do next?

11 Find these words in your dictionary. What are they in your language?

   transformer   metal

After you read

12 Who is speaking? Who to? Why do they say this?

   a "What! It's bigger! How did that happen?"

   b "Hit him again!"

   c ". . . what are you thinking? You can't go outside. It's dangerous."

13 Mr. Mars gives money to Joe, the Fimples, and the Abernathys.

   a Why does he do this?

   b Why doesn't he give money to Larry and Irwin?

Writing

14 Stuart, Irwin, Larry, and Mr. Mars have different ideas about toys. Write about them. What do you think?

15 You are Christy. Write a letter to Brad. Tell him that you do/do not want to see him again. Why?

16 The Gorgonites arrived in your country by boat, and you talked to them. They think your country is Gorgon! Write about your conversation for the newspaper.

17 Did you enjoy this story? Why/why not?

Answers for the Activities in this book are published in our free resource packs for teachers, the Penguin Readers Factsheets, or available on a separate sheet. Please write to your local Pearson Education office or to: Marketing Department, Penguin Longman Publishing, 5 Bentinck Street, London W1M 5RN.